# The Día de Los Muertos Story

## Celebrating the Never-Ending Bonds of Family

Andrea Jáuregui De La Torre

Illustrated by Laura González

becker&mayer! kids

In Aztec tradition, the souls of the dead return as butterflies, and if you see a hummingbird, it means that a loved one is sending you a message. Butterflies, especially monarchs, and hummingbirds also travel to Mexico for the winter, just in time to celebrate Día de Los Muertos!

*Xoloitzcuintles* (Xolos for short, and getting their name from Xolotl, the god of lightning, and *itzcuintli*, which means "dog") are Mexican dogs that the Aztecs believed were humankind's best friends not only in this life, but also in the afterlife. Xolos guide the souls of the dead through the underworld and help them find their loved ones on Día de Los Muertos.

**Count how many butterflies, hummingbirds, and Xolos you can find as you read the story!**

To my love, Joe. Thank you for supporting my every dream.

And to my Mexico—all the beauty I saw as a child, from *mercaditos* to volcanoes.

The story of Día de Los Muertos starts thousands of years ago. It is a beautiful and complicated tale filled with different cultures and traditions that have been passed down for many generations.

Día de Los Muertos means "Day of the Dead" in Spanish, but it is not a scary or sad day. It is the greatest family reunion, a serious but happy celebration where the living come together to remember those who have died and welcome their spirits home to visit.

People living in Mexico and Mexicans around the world honor their dead in many meaningful ways. Every family has a different and special way of celebrating the lives of those who have passed on, and it is through love that the memory of those who are gone lives on.

The history of Día de Los Muertos starts in ancient Mexico. Between 1300-1500 AD, the great civilization of the Aztecs ruled what is now central Mexico. They were an amazing people who believed in many gods and had lots of traditions and beliefs.

One of these traditions was to celebrate death; the Aztecs had parties for the dead about six times a year! Since they thought of death as an important part of life, they didn't fear the dead. They remembered and honored them.

Important Aztec celebrations were Miccailhuitontli (Feast of the Little Dead Ones), which honored children who had passed away, and Hueymiccaihuitl (Feast of the Departed Adults). For these feast days, the Aztecs would gather flowers to decorate their temples the night before and cook foods for the banquets on the day of the celebrations. They also would give gifts to gods like Huitzilopochtli, Tezcatlipoca, and many others in the name of those who had moved on in death.

Historians are unsure of exactly when these Aztec feasts for the dead started, but they could be connected to the Olmec people, who lived about 3,000 years ago around Mexico's Gulf Coast.

In 1519, the Spanish *conquistador* (explorer) Hernán Cortés and his crew arrived on Mexico's Gulf Coast and made their way into the city of Tenochtitlán (modern-day Mexico City). The Aztecs, who had lived in Tenochtitlán for hundreds of years, were surprised by these newcomers who believed they had a right to claim the land for themselves.

The Spanish also saw it as their duty to teach the Aztecs about their religion—Catholicism, a Christian faith—and to make them change their beliefs. This is how Christianity spread throughout the world, and how new practices replaced many native beliefs and traditions. Just like the Aztecs, Catholics have feasts for the dead. They believe that people who die can go to Heaven and become saints.

On November 1, Catholics celebrate All Saints' Day. Catholics believe people can become saints after they have done many great things for their communities when they were alive and continue to do so after their death through the power of God. To celebrate this day, many Catholic children dress up as their favorite saint.

On November 2, Catholics celebrate All Souls' Day to remember everyone who has died and is still on their afterlife journey. On this day, Catholics remember all the souls who may still be in purgatory (the stop before Heaven) by visiting the resting places of their dead and preparing meals in honor of those who have passed.

As time passed, some of the Aztec practices mixed in with Catholic rituals and new traditions were created. One of these new traditions is Día de Los Muertos, a beautiful day of remembrance that includes a little bit of both cultures.

Today, Día de Los Muertos is the time of the year when we welcome back our loved ones who have died. We look forward to their annual visits and honor them through happy celebrations.

Día de Los Muertos is family time. Family includes those who have lived before us and who we will never meet, but what ties family together through generations is our love for each other and the traditions we share.

We prepare for the holiday by getting our homes ready for our visitors by cleaning and creating an area for our *ofrendas*—our offerings for the dead.

We want to have the best space possible for our loved ones, so we sweep the floor, clean the windows, move furniture to make more space for celebrations, and start making decorations like *papel picado*. These are sheets of colorful paper cut into fun designs and come from an Aztec tradition of cutting and decorating paper they made from tree bark.

The *altar de muertos* is one of the most recognizable images of the Día de Los Muertos holiday. It's a special place where families collect their loved one's favorite things to create the ofrenda. The altar is a beautiful way to honor those who are gone but not forgotten and a reflection of the special relationship between the living and the dead.

On most altars, you'll find the four elements: a cup of water, candles to represent fire, food from the earth, and papel picado to represent air. We add personal items and pictures of departed loved ones along with candles to light the way home. Salt and a cross are added to purify the visiting souls, and we burn incense to protect against uninvited spirits.

Altars have either one, two, or three levels. A simple, one-level altar can have everything on display using a regular table like a dining or coffee table; a two-level altar can symbolize the difference between Earth and Heaven; and a three-level altar could include purgatory.

Food is a delicious and important part of the Día de Los Muertos celebration. It feeds the traveling ancestors and is also enjoyed by those honoring them. We use food as part of the ofrenda at home, and many choose to bring it to the cemetery as well.

Many traditional foods are enjoyed, like *conchas* (Mexican sweet bread), *pan de muertos* (a special holiday bread with a cross decoration), *mole* (a traditional sauce made with chiles and chocolate), *tamales* (corn dough filled with meat or cheese and wrapped in corn husks), *frutas* (fruits), and *frijoles* (beans). We also include the foods that our departed loved ones liked the most!

*Calaveritas* (small skulls) are also part of the delicious offerings. Made from sugar and decorated with colorful frosting, they offer a gentle way to view the departed—not as something scary, but as a part of our lives.

One of the most beautiful parts of the Día de Los Muertos celebration is the symbolic *cempasúchil* (marigold), a beautiful orange flower. The cempasúchil represents both light and brightness but also reminds us that all life eventually ends, and that is OK!

Across Mexico, parks and buildings are decorated with cempasúchils for the holiday. Cempasúchil garlands are used as part of ofrendas and to cover graves, and the flowers are also carried in cemetery processions or parades. We'll fill baskets with cempasúchils and place them around our house or wherever we gather to remember the deceased.

We place the cempasúchils around the departed's favorite objects or make petal paths to lead the way home. The bright orange color of the cempasúchil guides the souls of the dead toward their living relatives, and the strong and pleasant smell of the flower lets the spirits know it is safe to visit.

Día de Los Muertos has many symbols—things that mean something else and that help us remember something important.

During Día de Los Muertos, you may notice a very tall and noble skeleton lady. This is La Catrina, a strong figure in Mexican culture and an important symbol of the holiday!

Some believe La Catrina represents the Aztec goddess of death, Mictecacīhuatl, watching over us, while others say she is just a character created by artist José Guadalupe Posada.

In 1910, Posada drew his La Catrina cartoon to help everyone remember that no matter who you are, what you look like, or what you have, everyone meets death. La Catrina is also a reminder not to be sad when people die, as we will see our loved ones again someday.

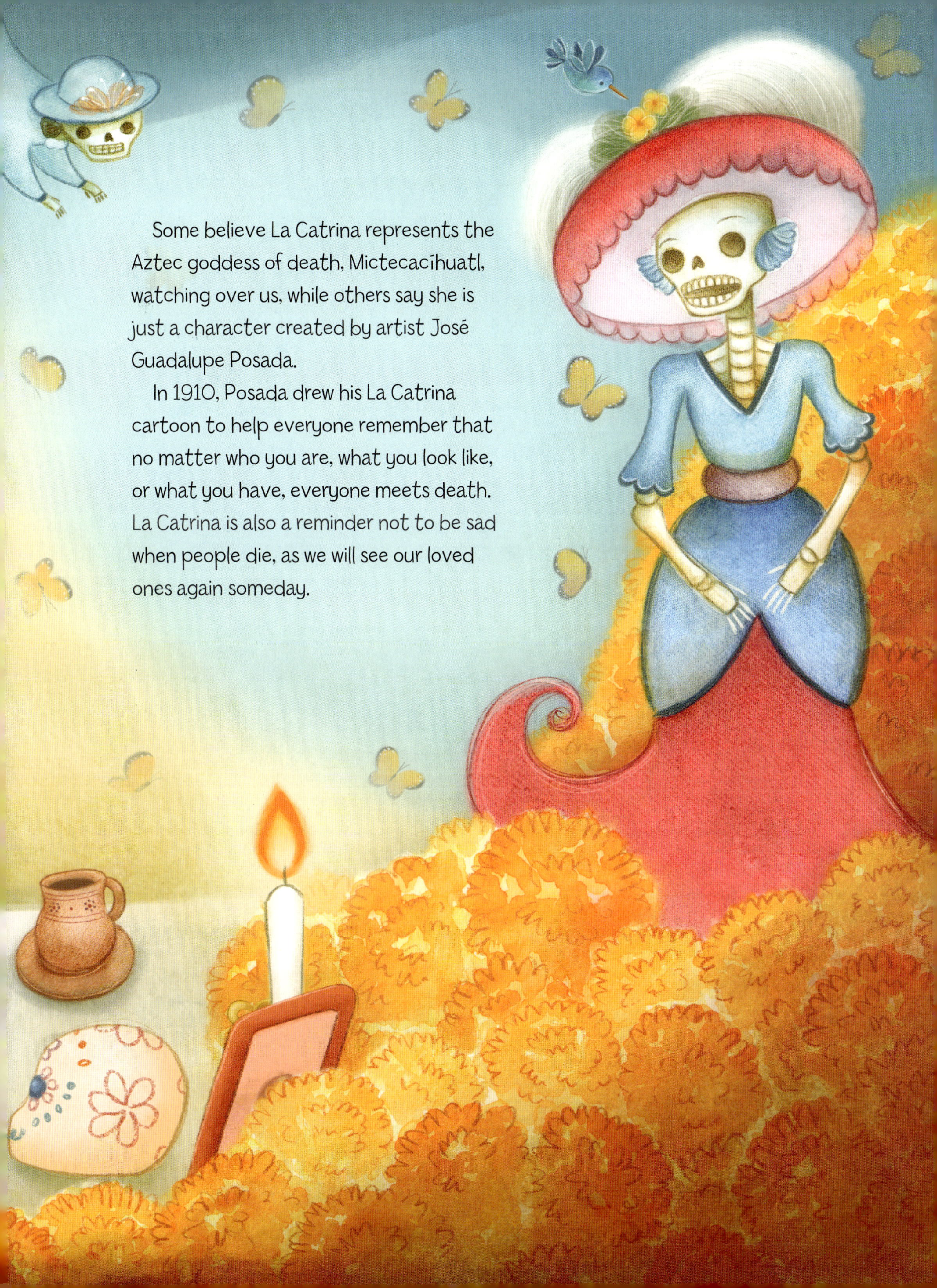

Many families choose to visit their deceased loved ones at their graves during Día de Los Muertos. Family members arrive in candlelit processions, praying or singing, thinking of their lost relatives.

We clean the graves and then bring cempasúchils and candles to decorate them with the beautiful orange color and warming light to welcome the spirits home.

Together as a family, we eat and drink all the yummy treats of the holiday and tell happy stories about those who have passed on. We bring our own instruments or full mariachi bands to play songs for everyone. It is a time of love and joy when we celebrate the coming together of many generations of family members, connecting the past to the present.

We celebrate Día de Los Muertos around the same time of the year as other similar holidays—All Saints' Day, All Souls' Day, and one that is *very* famous in the United States: Halloween! Because new traditions are always being created, many Mexican children today visit neighbors to ask for calaveritas, similar to trick or treating. But it is important to remember that every holiday is special in its own way!

While these holidays are connected, Día de Los Muertos is its own important time to remember, honor, and celebrate the people we love who have passed on from this life. It's a joyful and festive time when we do not fear the dead, but instead invite them to come visit us. It is a happy time that reminds us of the never-ending bonds of family, and that while those who we love may leave us in life, they are never really gone because love lasts forever.

# Timeline

The Día de Los Muertos holiday is now part of life in the United States thanks to our Mexican ancestors bringing their traditions with them when immigrating. Today, many Mexican communities include the traditions that they grew up with or that their grandparents brought with them in their celebrations. Many families in America choose to celebrate Día de Los Muertos and the Catholic holidays instead of Halloween, but other families and communities choose to take bits of each tradition and have as many parties as possible around the end of October and the beginning of November. These family traditions have spread beyond the walls of homes as big US cities, like San Diego, San Antonio, Albuquerque, New Orleans, and Chicago, host well-attended Día de Los Muertos festivities and events every year, including exhibitions, feasts, and parades or processions, inviting everyone in the community from all backgrounds to be part of the celebration.

**1500 AC–100 AD** The ancient Olmec civilization holds feasts for their dead to show great respect for death and to celebrate it as life's next passage.

**609 AD** Pope Boniface IV begins All Saints' Day in Rome to celebrate Catholic saints on November 1. Saints are special people who have done good works in life and after death through the power of God..

**837 AD** Pope Gregory IV makes All Saints' Day an official holiday of the Catholic Church.

**1048 AD** A Catholic priest, Abbot Saint Odilo of Cluny, establishes All Souls' Day on November 2—a day for Catholics to remember all those who have died.

**1345 AD–1521 AD** Aztecs rule in Mesoamerica (modern-day Mexico) and have feasts for their dead, some around the middle of autumn.

**1519 AD** Spanish conquistador Hernán Cortés arrives in Mexico to claim the land for Spain and brings with him All Saints' Day, All Souls' Day, and other Catholic and Christian religious traditions.

**1910** Artist José Guadalupe Posada draws the iconic skeleton lady La Catrina, an important symbol of Mexico and Día de Los Muertos.

**1924** Mexican artist Diego Rivera paints the mural *Dream of a Sunday Afternoon in Alameda Central Park (Sueño de una tarde dominical en la Alameda Central)*, featuring La Catrina and his wife, fellow artist Frida Kahlo, who also used well-known Día de Los Muertos images in her art.

**1970s** Mexicans introduce Día de Los Muertos to their communities in California cities as a way of cultural expression and to reclaim Indigenous heritage.

**2008** UNESCO reflects the importance of the holiday by adding Mexico's "Indigenous festivity dedicated to the dead" to its list of Intangible Cultural Heritage of Humanity.

**2014** 20th Century Fox releases the animated movie, *The Book of Life*, that celebrates Día de Los Muertos and introduces young audiences from different backgrounds to the holiday.

**2015** The James Bond movie *Spectre* features a large Day of the Dead parade, marking a major moment for the holiday in pop culture.

**2016** Mexico City holds its first parade for Día de Los Muertos.

**2017** Several major cities across the US hold Day of the Dead parades.

**2017** Disney and Pixar release the animated movie, *Coco*, celebrating the Mexican tradition of connecting with ancestors. The movie further increases the popularity of the holiday worldwide.

**Today** Día de Los Muertos is celebrated around the world, recognized as a mixture of Mexico's history and family tradition.

# My Día de Los Muertos Connection

Día de Los Muertos to me shows the beauty of Mexico, an enormous land, naturally rich with an incredibly diverse collection of landscapes. In Mexico, you can visit *cenotes* (limestone sinkholes), impressive canyons, active volcanoes, gorgeous shores, snowy mountains, waterfalls, jungles, and more! And Mexico's culture of family, love, music, and togetherness can be seen in all corners of the country.

Día de Los Muertos is a holiday that amplifies a need for community that Mexicans have held onto since birth. Families gather for *carne asadas* (barbeques) almost every weekend and religious sacraments are huge family celebrations.

I haven't lived in Mexico for a few years now, but the memories of my childhood there are bright and warm, especially when I remember Día de Los Muertos and celebrating it in different parts of the country. As a child, I don't think I truly understood that we were talking about a sad topic: Everything felt like a celebration! I remember my mom telling me about my grandparents and celebrating their lives at the San Miguel de Allende parades. It's all a flurry of colorful memories for me, but what stands out the most is a feeling of belonging.

I remember studying the parts of the ofrenda in my Catholic school, seeing the inviting orange color of the cempasúchil around my neighborhood, and the feeling of community gathering together. I specifically remember walking around the cobbled streets of San Miguel de Allende, seeing the giant *catrinas* (skeletons) on stilts and cempasúchils everywhere. I remember walking past beautiful, barred windows and peeking in to see the ofrendas facing toward the street with their black and white family pictures surrounded by food and joyful colors.

My favorite part was eating the calaveritas. My two sisters and I would each get to pick one (I always picked the brightest color), and it was so fun to take off the sequined eyes before eating all the sugar. Our parents would warn us that our stomachs would hurt . . . and they always did!

I got married ten years ago back in San Miguel de Allende, in the church where my grandparents are buried. We processed through the town with *mojigangas* (giant puppets), and I felt so connected to my country. Flashes of Día de Los Muertos parades went through my mind as I looked around at all my loved ones. These types of traditions hold Mexicans together and show the world our culture's richness.

I love that I can pass this tradition down to my children and that they can be a part of generations who view and celebrate death in a healthy way. We set an altar for my deceased grandparents and make pan de muertos and calaveritas so that they can experience the holiday through food like I did.

Every year since my first son was born, we've thrown a huge party for my friends and neighbors at the end of October. It is usually a Halloween party but also an All Saints' Day celebration where I use Día de Los Muertos decorations and themes to help my American friends learn more about the holiday.

My favorite part of Día de Los Muertos is that it's a holiday that holds so much history and culture that can be shared in such a fun way with others.

**What's your Día de Los Muertos connection, and how will you celebrate?**

First published in 2025 by becker&mayer!kids,
an imprint of The Quarto Group,
135 West 36th Street, 13th Floor,
New York, NY 10018, USA
(212) 779-4972
www.Quarto.com

EEA Representation, WTS Tax d.o.o.,
Žanova ulica 3, 4000 Kranj, Slovenia.
www.wts-tax.si



10 9 8 7 6 5 4 3 2 1

ISBN: 979-8-3179-0275-9

Library of Congress Control Number: 2026937296

Group Publisher: Rage Kindelsperger
Creative Director: Laura Drew
Managing Editor: Cara Donaldson
Art Director: Scott Richardson
Cover and Interior Design: Scott Richardson

Printed in Huizhou City, Guangdong, China TT062026

Lexile® NC1270L